SPECTATOR

Spectator

KARA CANDITO

THE AGHA SHAHID ALI PRIZE IN POETRY

THE UNIVERSITY OF UTAH PRESS
Salt Lake City

THE AGHA SHAHID ALI PRIZE IN POETRY
SERIES EDITOR: Katharine Coles
ADVISORY EDITOR: Jacqueline Osherow

The Defiance House Man colophon is a registered trademark of the University of Utah Press. It is based on a four-foot-tall Ancient Puebloan pictograph (late PIII) near Glen Canyon, Utah.

18 17 16 15 14   1 2 3 4 5

LIBRARY OF CONGRESS CATALOGING-IN-PUBLICATION DATA
Candito, Kara.
  [Poems. Selections]
  Spectator / Kara Candito.
    pages ; cm
  ISBN 978-1-60781-351-4 (pbk. : alk. paper)
  ISBN 978-1-60781-352-1 (ebook)
  I. Title.
  PS3603.A537A6 2014
  811'.6—dc23

                        2014007893

ON THE COVER: *Olympia* by Beth Cavener. Used by permission.

For Victor—mil gracias for crossing over

CONTENTS

IV.

I.

INITIATION #5: LORCA

He is standing at the foot of my bed
with an insanely tragic smile and a syringe
full of lead. He is sitting beside me
in a bloodless body, stroking the pink sheets
with eyes like a fruit that's never in season.
Burning casinos and countries I'll never visit
pass over the room. I am here
to learn how to suffer more beautifully.
Outside, at the bus stop, thin men in scrubs
read about nanobots, and maybe they can map
the malignant cells unspooling in my marrow,
or the best, fastest path of a bullet entering the chest.
Inside, in another dimension, we are riding
two lame mares to the pasture where I am
ravaged by centaur after centaur, never a satyr.
Bodies matter, how they break open,
which animals we let inside us. I am here
to learn how to suffer more beautifully,
to smile for the white air and give everything away.

A SHORT GENEALOGY OF POWER TOOLS

There was this shed behind the prefab house
   where I straddled a boy named Boomer
on his father's John Deere. Into the shaved back
of his head, I dug my nails to pretend they were
      power tools; my hands blasting
his body open, so I could crawl inside and make it mine.

But afterward, when the mulch smelled feral
   and the wheelbarrow looked like an exhausted animal,
and I had to pee, there was just this total annoyance
with being back in my body, with being a person
      of dumb, particular needs, suddenly
waving *hello* to his mother, who called
   the bathroom a *powder room*, which was a sad
suburban lie that cut me anyway.
And the soap was sharp and the shower curtain
was sharp and I was wearing a white sweatshirt.
      And the face in the mirror was the worst

kind of moralist. It said: *You cannot invent a thing*
   with wires and blades and call it a coronation.
I want to tell you this without saying that my mother's car
was already in the driveway; that shoulder pads
      and brass buttons made her look like a man;
that when she squinted and said, *Stop being so goddamn sullen,*
      she was one. And breathing became
this nameless, miraculous crime.

CREATION MYTH, 1979 (REAPPROPRIATED)

Apprentice of the deadpan entrance—born on Labor Day,
two weeks late, plopped onto the lap of a heat wave; the doctor
        dragged off the tenth hole; your father sobbing
in the waiting room, cigars stillborn in the box. *The firstborn should be a son.*
        9½ months earlier, his youngest brother, stranded
on I-95 in a blizzard, shelled his last pistachio, unfastened his seatbelt
        and sank into the giddy, dreamless sleep of a toddler—

        his last thought an abandoned mineshaft where mussel shell fossils
and cypress trees brand the blasted walls. At the same moment
        in a duplex in Quincy, the oblivious seams of your
parents' sighs as they rolled back and forth in front of the fire
        with "A Case of You" blaring on the battery-powered radio,
clothes crammed inside a military-issue sleeping bag;
        the roof already buckling beneath snow and ice.

        White waves breaking over the wall at Nantasket, white waves
of sex and sleep, all that is numb and holy. Only a child conceived
        in a killing blizzard could love the jagged elegies of frost
on the highway, could watch the same clip of a senator shooting himself
        in the mouth over and over, mesmerized by the alchemy
of objects—the state seal on the wall, an organ donor card facedown
        on the podium, the camera panning in on the exit wound.

        You were meant for that immaculate spectacle,
a halo of blood and tissue. Nothing still, nothing whole.
        Past and future pinned there, like a dentist's chair

where the hygienist administers nitrous like a drunken sergeant—
the needle throbbing through the gum, the needle
withdrawn. Laughing when it feels like half your face is gone.

FAMILY ELEGY IN A LATE STYLE OF FIRE

In the story no one tells, my Great Uncle Salvatore
is an errand boy for the mafiosi and ends up on the dance floor

of Cocoanut Grove in Boston, November, 1942, an hour
before the club ignites; this is one version of justice.

Now Levis would say that fire is *so American*. We know
he drank until all that remained of his world was a match

trembling down a dark motel hall—the flame
finite and manageable—while behind the bolted doors

of every room on the floor little Neros played embossed
harps muttering *E tu, ignis, e tu*? And it's true, I'd rather drown

than burn, but the best death is undoubtedly getting lost
in a blizzard. Frost spends whole books stumbling through

snowy woods, though he never mentions how he ends up
in them, or how he gets out alive. Deer have been known

to swim out to sea without reason, and though the dumbest
end up as road kill, I'll put my faith in the long distance swimmers,

the Aeneases that wash up on strange shores and found
profane cities. Like fire and water, facts are tireless.

His last few months Salvatore bought jewels no one in Reggio
could imagine, and never wore them. One is a saint's knuckle

cast in 18-carat gold. My grandfather keeps it in a backlit shadowbox.
In my drawer, there's a blood-coral cornuto because the dead

will play the same dirge in the dark for years. And what
is more haunted than the feathery music of fire?

This November, I'll get it right. I won't imagine Salvatore
and the revolving door jammed with bodies, or the flashover's

chemical boom, like an ancient tomb stunned open.
I'll go back to Calabria and find myself at fourteen, reading

a mystery novel under a bergamot tree. I might miss TV.
I might be extravagantly bored. I might talk about churches

where no one is lighting candles for dead relatives.
Whose stage are you on? Whose pyre are you in? I'll ask myself,

knowing I have to become someone else to answer this.
If, in the end, we get what we pay for, then I would like a receipt,

please. If, in the end, the band is playing "Bell Bottom Trousers,"
let that be his favorite song. Let him wade onto the dance floor,

into the slack-tide of a forgotten life. Let him—

UPON SEEING SIMON & GARFUNKEL
LIVE AT THE COLISEUM

We're sweating, the pecorino's
sweating. This pergola of wires is our mother.
There'll be no more dying in the Borghese,
she says, or in the piazzas airbrushed with Bellinis.
We'll undress in the same spot where gladiators
head-butted for the emperor's amusement,
and there'll be no more diplomacy, just streaking
through the ruins until the buried bathhouses
are born again on the Via Corso and Love
itself swaggers down the Spanish Steps,
like a Keatsian vision.

Sure, last summer, when the temperature
rose to 104, Russian tourists fainted in the Pantheon
and vomit ran down the stones like rainwater
or the blood of traitors. But look how we've
survived, better dressed and sentimental;
swaying, saluting a half moon as the Ideal
descends upon us—a piccolo trumpet,
a baby Aston Martin.

Tomorrow, young fathers will sleep off
the grappa on trains to Portofino. Children
will swim out too far while their obscenely
beautiful mothers read *fotoromanzi* in linen dresses,
and the lanky cabana boys will be smitten,
just as I am when a pointy-chinned Macedonian
asks, *Che e' 'homeward bound'?*

But I can't explain it. Mercury,
god of travel, shape-shifting, and alchemy,
I want too much to conquer you. To read Montale
on a balcony besieged by almond trees, to cry
into my macchiato in an airport lounge,
is all one wish; the traveler's backward look.
Tomorrow, I'll board a plane for New York.
I'm twenty-three. My skin and my Italian
are as perfect as they'll ever be.

A GENEALOGY OF THE FATHER

I.

Everything I know about silence I learned
the morning of September 11th trying
to reach my father on his cell in lower Manhattan.
No one got through.
When he finally called
       there was nothing to say except
You're still there. And all in all,
I think of *there* as a treeless island
where a secret is buried in wet sand.
       If the ferry is full, I'll swim.
       If I drown, I drown.

II.

"If you are Calabrian, the ocean is in your blood,"
says my father, poetic for once. Then, he yanks
the lawnmower cord, and everywhere headless
dandelions; the wrong, sweet smell of cut grass
        blowing across the yard before I exist.

III.

I mean before he is my father and therefore
indentured; before the 70s when the Atlantic is toxic
and humpback whales wash up on Nantasket Beach
       dead, fat, and full of algae;
before he builds Boston Whalers and returns
to my mother each night with fiberglass
under his fingernails; before he buys
a sailboat he can't afford, stencils *Cara Mia*
across the hull and runs private cruises
from Miami to Martinique, Saint Lucia, Curacao—
islands we'd visit on a cruise ship in ten years
       and ask *land or water excursion?*—
before the 80s and the drug pirates;
before my father auctions the boat,
sells insurance policies and drinks
his vermouth neat each night watching
the news cycle unfurl like a mooring line,

IV.

it is Boston, 1966—

      is there ever an innocent year?
My parents meet at a Catholic high school
named after the saint of lost objects.

      Latin class, genitive case:
my father is the Calabrian milkman's son.
He scrubs toilets to pay tuition.
His collars are furiously starched.
His voice is parched, savage, smiling.
"Like the *mezzogiorno*," says my mother,
who had never been to Italy.

      Amor fati.
Like Nietzsche, I do not want to accuse.

V.

"A section of your book will be the Father's,"
the poet augurs. Biblical, Jungian, Lacanian—
the Father. Can I call him that and me *you*?

VI.

These things are dear to the Father in 1991:
a mason jar of rare sea glass on his dresser;
a miniature replica of a Sicilian fishing boat
on the mantle; a set of Callaway golf clubs.
When the Father returns from work
in a skyscraper twenty miles away,
you're folding laundry, rolling his sweat socks
into fist-sized balls. It's funny really,
a pure joy, a joke when you aim and hurl
a pair at him (he never taught you to play catch),
then miss, strike the tiny bow. The sail snaps,
the ship goes down. Splendid, ridiculous,
the Father forging the room like a channel.
When he was four his uncle threw him
off the end of the pier at high tide and called it
learning to swim.

      The Father slaps your stunned cheek,
not hard, but the amplified crack,
like a wave striking the side of a ship;
not hard, but you're triumphant now,
contact-drunk, both of you awash
in the tidal pull of performance.
So you say it, the worst insult in his language,
words reserved for men and their enemies:
      I hope you outlive your children.
Neither of you ever mention this.
Not the next day when a nor'easter shreds
the coast with twenty-five-foot waves,
sucks whole houses and hotels into the sea
from Marshfield, to North Beach, to Brant Point.
Because it is October and no longer hurricane season,
      the storm is never named.

VII.

When I am eight and want *more than anything in the world*
an absurd green raft in the shape of a crocodile,
my father looks me in the eye right in the aisle of Caldor
          and asks, "How does it feel to want?"

VIII.

How does it feel? Here, the male poet
finds a sheltered inlet, drops anchor
and muses—for years, he drifted,
distant, drunk, dear/detested dad;
hardy, leaky, forever bobbing
out past channel, while I, on shore
with brother and fishing rod; my not-yet
beard and public library card,
waited. For years he drifted,
      until one day dad ran aground—
sober, dead, in diapers.
Now, I'm older. We've become
one falling body, dad and I,
by which I mean we love and hate
our wives. In dreams, we go off
      to sea (as metaphor) together,
      and rest on our weary oars.

IX.

"His uncle helped him build it, then he died,"
says my nonna the fatalist when I find
my father's pinewood derby car in the basement.

      Is this sequence causal? Arbitrary? Predetermined?
I want to learn more and more to see as beautiful
what is necessary in things. Resolution
      of shadow and noon.

X.

The same dream—I'm reading or watching TV
in a hotel bed when a man I've slept with,
am sleeping with, crawls in beside me,
lowers himself delicately, as if the bed
were perched on a cliff and beneath it
open water. We don't speak. The weight settles,
the parts settle—his bare skin against my stomach.
We don't speak when he peels back the blankets,
shows me the cuts covering his arms,
his shoulders, his neck. They make him look
like a crownless Spanish Inquisition Christ,
and looking is like swimming out so far
that the shore could be anywhere—
backward, forward, another horizon.
The cuts are symmetrical, intentional.
This is a clean operation. He turns
to me and says very quietly:
        "Look how I've suffered for you."

II.

ARS POETICA #9 (THE AFTER-HOURS VERSION)
After Terrance Hayes

My husbands smile like mystics and prophets
and bandits. They think the number eleven is holy.
My husbands blush when they try to say
sadness in Italian. They sit cross-legged on the carpet
pretending to read my poems. One
of my husbands wants to be a surgeon. One
wants to be a cadaver. Another weeps
twice a week for his incurable disease. My husband,
Mr. I-can't-sleep-without-the-television-on,
tells me I'm as pretty as Italy, but he's never
left the country. Here is the gold necklace
another husband gave me after he made me cry
in an airport. My husband, the Mexican sculptor,
turns my wine corks into trays then says,
"Mi amor, you have a drinking problem."
Each of my husbands asks, "Am I the best
husband you've ever had?" They worship sex.
No, they worship answers more than sex.
We are reading the *Gypsy Ballads*, my husbands
and me, and there are fountains and scabbed-
over moons and civil guards. There are
crystal tambourines and words that gleam
like silverware. But my husbands are bored.
Some of them sing arias in the shower.
Some of them type their secrets into a computer.
My husbands take turns undressing me

in the cheapest rooms of a hotel by the sea.
We are tourists at heart, my husbands and me;
we ask the wrong questions,
then fall asleep with the lights on.

EPITHALAMIUM INTERCEPTED AT THE BORDER

Cairo, 2006

Every morning, the waiter in a tarboosh. Every morning,
      Sahadi honey on flatbread. Every morning you teach me
a new word. *Bokrah* means *tomorrow* and the Ptolemy's inbred tombs.
      Bokrah, our engagement dinner with your parents,
    your mother gaping over Circassian chicken: *Her American accent!*
      So many words are forbidden, so I sing in the shower.
I picture God, Allah, Krishna, and Jupiter arguing at the bottom
      of the Nile. *No God but God!* they shout underwater.
No God but God, and your mother, His campaign manager.
      And your father, His cripple maker. We are
His Ponzi scheme, His wish for infinite wishes. I wish to crawl
      inside the Colossus of Ramses, to clutch a bouquet
of arrows in the afterlife. Picture us. Picture the Messiah's
      nanny stacking gift receipts in the manger. He whose name
we are forbidden to mention *on pain of death*. So, write it in white ink—
      fourteen wet dreams in the Dead Sea, forty quickies in the desert,
    400 years of heretic sound effects in the feral garden
      on the mountain where Moses fattens up his pigeons.
So it is written that I welcome the messenger's sickle-sharp tongue
      (We cut whom we love) and sleep the whole flight home
with a diamond ring burning in my checked bag, a copper halo sinking over Cairo,
      and your name—my trembling cup, overturned.

BESTIARY

I consider the famous poet's majesty when he recites
      an ode to my ass—Left Bank beret askew on the alopecia,
          an expired visa, sardonic deployment of Dada.
After the reading, holding court in the chiaroscuro,
      partaking of éclairs and smoked scotch—
              Is this tasteless? he asks.
Yes, though we have a kind of alliance,
      his come-ons for my silence; his bouquet of internet memes
          for my—how to say?—*proximity*, as in the documentary
where a man lives among Kodiak bears and gets eaten.
          As in, of course I get in the car and he blasts
              "Giant Steps" all the way to the pier—
why not admit that the weather is, at least, panegyric?
      With his Zippo aglow, he speaks of a wife whose name
          might be Vera, who might be a surrealist reporter,
a connoisseur of vodka, omnivorous in her housedress.
          One hand touring the ecotone of my back, he mimics
              Khrushchev, he makes himself laugh,
and I remember a family trip to Fort Lauderdale, the marina
      where my father admired other men's
          boats. I never spoke there either, a pure spectator,
though manatees swam beneath our feet, so free
      I wanted to smash a fist beneath the surface.
              One's back had been cut by a propeller.
Is this scary? it seemed to cry, *Would you like to join me?*
      I did not reply. Was that tasteless? Was that an invitation?
      Does silence mean consent? Too many highballs,

bottom-feeders, one-liners. It's like sitting at the stern
              of a glass-bottom boat watching blowfish,
                        how they devour chunks of cheap white bread.

LORCA'S LAST LETTER TO DALÍ, AUGUST 20, 1936

> *You do well when you post warning flags*
> *Along the dark limit that shines in the night.*
> — Frederico García Lorca, "Ode to Salvador Dalí"

What part of your dream logic will tell you
      I wasn't looking for science or your cock?
I stumbled into the orchard with my hands bound

and my pockets stuffed with bitter oranges. The Law
      is an affectation. Its roots are bare wires.
The mind reaches only as far as the fingers. Today

I am *map, grove, moan;* a boy in cold bathwater crying,
      father! I play pallet to the frozen aqueduct
of your wrist, which is a firing squad, the shallow

grave where I bleed beside a matador and an old
      schoolteacher, his beard full of famished doves.
Tonight in Cadiz, the fortune-teller wears a collar

of bees and horse thieves turn bacchanals into lullabies
      outside the walls of the city. Am I the death mask
every gypsy boy clutches to his chest? If forgiveness

is a smile of bullets, then my name means *antiseptic*
      and it will sting each time you touch a paintbrush.
There is no one who can sing without hearing

the cries of pinned olive trees. There is no one
      who can say we did not lie side by side, tucked
into the twin coffins of our lives while Spain

emptied its ashtrays into our mouths.

LORCA RECALLS HIS FIRST LOVE

Like an albino Apollo, the stable boy I loved
one summer is digging my horse's grave
all afternoon in the woods behind the orchard,

shirtless and short of breath; the sun wringing
clouds from the three o'clock sky; the scars
from his father's riding crop branching across

his back like the tangled script of a riddle I
refused to answer. His face, a maze of tears,
anonymous now, as the rooms of a disgraced palace

where the walls are hung with the laws of conquered
empires and servants distill arak in the kitchen,
whispering about the sultan's fatal condition.

Imagine my pale boy on his knees in a straw hat;
the first fist of dirt tossed onto the shrouded horse.
Imagine a river throbbing through the ravine below—

marrow of bone, sap of tree—and flowers, not
funereal, but lavender and jasmine, the sky speckled
with the cries of migrating swallows. A Moorish wind

wiping us clean, wiping the cypress trees clean, until
there is no such thing as man or woman. Just sweat
and the astringent smell of lemons. Two boys

with wildflowers behind their ears; the tangled flag
of a fallen nation—my tongue on his pearled shoulder,
an Act of Contrition.

LORCA ADDRESSES HIS SISTER BEFORE HER WEDDING

Someone has promised you two mute red bulls
        and tender veronicas. Little cakes on the table and sugar
caught in your throat every morning until you die.

Now, mother sticks thorns in the brims of straw hats
        and your breasts fill the kitchen window like clenched flowers,
or the moans of *cante jondo:* bride, silver, sadness—

the words hide their faces in your hair, sister. So stay
        here in the yard with me while wives forget the fall
of Icarus, just as I, for days on end, refused to cry

for the hawthorn tree, its trunk defaced by ten daggers,
        and Mother at the hearth stumbling through
her rosary. The saints hide their faces in your hair, sister.

So stay here at the piano with me and tap a spoon in your
        palm while I play "The Smuggler's Song." *Who will buy*
from me some black thread? My horse is tired. I run beside it.

At dawn, the Great Suicides will tell you they are just bones
        and buttons in the secular ground. So, walk with me
by the river, all anise and silver, where you can dance

like a condemned Artemis, unspeakably dressed,
        plucking the conjugal arrows from your breasts.
Throw that ring in the water! Sing with me, sister,

before dawn's fermata cloisters your open throat.

BY THE NUMBERS

January. Calculable velocity of 1
regional jet crossing the sudden
starless 40 miles west of Detroit
1400 miles north of you with 12
exotic birds in the cargo hold.
On the starboard side a dry half-moon
20,000 feet above Lake Michigan.
Here it is permissible to wonder
Color? Species? Country of origin?
It is permissible to think *call me*
no don't. Tiny doubts please
touch down and warm Diet Coke
in the seat-back pocket. Last night
licking the bars of our separate cages
we watched each other watching
the diminishing salt of hours.
Touch down *mi amor definintiva*
you said *déjame a year no more*
then we'll live together.
Here it is permissible to laugh
at the promises one lets sit
on the black tongue of the wing.
Everything in the off position now.
Here it is permissible to believe
the 12 birds existed
because the flight attendant
told us they were cold.

CAMINO REAL

After Joshua Clover

First it was one checkpoint and then it
was another checkpoint. On the highway
between D.F. & Puebla two federales

boarded the bus and ordered the women off.
We tend to think *not me,* or *just me.*
One wore an assault rifle across his back,

another pointed a video camera at our faces.
At these moments, we tend to think massacre,
as in no longer a number, or biopower,

as in Foucault's botched orgy visions.
The one with the assault rifle said
quite los lentes, and I was on my knees

as in prayer, the compliance position,
pure submission. The federales laughed,
and I was just another silly woman

on her knees at a checkpoint south
of a Volkswagen factory where Mexicans
manufacture German cars, as in

high performance engines; speed
management. Not bullets, but the red
record button; the mouth effaced

by the camera saying *rubia, linda,*
ojos verdes. To my left, a covered
well for animals. The assumption

is that the missing are dead or in safe
houses. The assumption as slippage
of language. To my right, the bus

where Victor watched me watching
the camera pan in on my face. Blue curtains,
the smell of animals and cooking oil.

We were, by this time, already leaving,
as in all this was no longer our problem—
checkpoints, surveillance, narco-terrorism,

the D.E.A. doctrine, species management.
Footage of Rodney King, Katrina,
Los Angeles, New Orleans, the National Guard.

We call it a *lifestyle decision*, these mornings
spent reading *El Norte* on our iPads,
studying the photos of headless bodies

hanging from bridges. Biopower—
a covered well for animals. The squinting
and trying not to piss oneself.

The *not me* of it, which is the final take.

V'S DREAM ON THE PLANE
FROM MEXICO CITY TO CHICAGO

It began with aduanas
and my mother's childhood name;
escalators, drug-sniffing dogs;
            you, the night wind cloaking Insurgentes
and riding a stolen bike past the blackened
            monuments of national heroes. I was following

Porfirio Díaz, but maybe he wasn't
Porfirio Díaz. It began in a public bathroom
with a dripping faucet where my mother
            and I hunched like animals in front of the urinals.
In the middle, a florescent lamp, tarmac, a torn
            tablecloth. The light moved

like a virus. In the middle, my mother
spat and rubbed her palms together—
an undersong of saliva and gardenia
            and *mijo never, never marry a gringa.*
In the middle, we crouched in the front
            of the urinals as if already

it were winter and we'd never stand
together again. Outside, snakes curled
beneath the nogal trees where
            the swallows were falling.
A tearing sound,

like two possible endings—
me voy, me voy,
con permiso. Now,
        something flies away,
or something is poisoned.

III.

TEN YEARS APPRENTICESHIP
IN THE REPUBLIC OF CARNIVOROUS LOVE

for Federico García Lorca

Horses harrow the trail to a little house where a guitar
with brittle strings waits for a boy who plays video games

in another country. You never kept a blog, so you can't know
how it feels to shoot blank flares onto a screen where every word

unfolds like chairs at a garish banquet. We've been to your
Garden of Lunar Grapefruits and turned it into a Facebook group.

Escarpment of weightless reverie, it still gleams, though we've
auctioned off the frogs and the fireflies. Granada has sold out, too;

a white wall, a blank white wall, the new-fangled hiss of a bus
delivering tourists to the Costa del Sol. Hernandez might've been

Spain's cell-block saint with his journals of tears and onion milk,
wrangling his grief into a single lullaby. But I'd rather ride bareback

with you, Federico, through a forest of imperious branches,
to that double lake where fish feed on motor oil and grief.

I've been too much the student, would drown myself
for the urgent pitch of a fair-use *Olé*, would swallow mouthfuls

of muck just to know what death felt like. Did life look dumb
and intimate, like a little drunken rider? Or, was it an empty saddle

and the whiteness of a horse bolted across a flattened field?

DYING IN AN EARTHQUAKE IN MEXICO CITY

It's not us. It's the universe
throwing us up. I used to have a lot
of trouble with verbs. I used to be
mystified by action.
     For example,
when you said *me entrego a ti*—
I heard, *I bury myself in you*,
so I imagined a shovel or a tomb
or a coffin, as in your cadaver
was there, but hidden. It was a question
of tone, a question of distance.
     Me entrego a ti—
I surrender, transfer, pay, deliver
(myself) to you. And when do the sirens start?
     Me entierro a ti—
I bury, forget, thrust (myself) into you,
into these words, onto the jagged
crescent of your chipped front tooth.
It's an adolescent story you told me
about a bike and a bottle of Jack Daniels.
It's the one story you told me when I said
     Tell me something interesting.
In other words: *Bury yourself.*
       Hand me an injury.

DEAR FORGIVENESS,

Remember when we met on OkCupid?
        You called the profile picture of me in scorpion pose
beneath a palmetto tree *playful* and *suggestive.*
                How long can you hold that? you asked, and for maybe two minutes
I was rare and witty, a smart romantic comedy.

Dear Forgiveness, I waited three hours
        for you at the corner table of a bistro renowned for its kale crisps.
When you didn't show up, I gave the world
                my phone number, I resorted to the usual shock-and-awe—
your empty chair like a burning acre;
my tongue like the cotton plugging an aspirin bottle.

Even before the headache arrived, I was treating it
        with blackout blinds or the caffeine cure. One vacancy
follows another; have you noticed? Pills plopped
                into a clammy palm—full-hollow things
as in hobbies or strong opinions.

Dear Forgiveness, I have found the missing footage
        of the little girl who got none.
I have gobbled all of the cherries you said we'd eat
                together. I have gobbled all of the consecrated fruits,
and I'm not sorry.

DEATHBED

If you think it's just another lurid metaphor,
            then I applaud your worldliness. But this is
      a bona fide deathbed, with ordinary, pilly sheets
shrouding my feet. This is the dim spot where my head
      rests like a comma between clauses,
where my hands flap together like parataxis.

In this life, my love for poems was all balled up in bluster,
            full of femme fatales and polyglot victims—
      the old arguments of who's screwing whom
and why and with what. Let's say I swallowed a Fellini film
      and spat it back up. I grew ugly. I encountered
metaphors at night, slumping in my chair

like a Chilean dictator renouncing all former ties
            to frivolous displays of power. Have you
      ever been embarrassed by a metaphor?
It is embarrassing to write. This is why I wear an expression
      of crude conviction, the one that made my mother say:
Stop making squinty faces. You'll get wrinkles.

So, no more poems. No more lyric I's to call the troops home
            from the confines of the pillowcases.
      No more gilded expeditions to the secret grove
where everyone groans and takes off their clothes. I want to be
      alone with my regrets, sophomoric as they may seem—
all of the writing and the writhing.

I want to reel in and out like an AM radio
        on an indigent nightstand. I want to reach out
    and turn the volume up just before I die.

ELEVATOR: A LOVE STORY

Someone says *a poem can't just plunge into*
surrealistic bewilderment no matter how much
your life sucks. Someone else says
the attempt to store or isolate momentum is tyranny.
These two things, and weeks spent deciphering
the elevator dream, though the setting is not
a casino-lit skybox in a high-end mall—
or a Halliburton safe house in which whole
countries are fucked between P4 and Mezzanine.
This is an ordinary elevator in the lobby
of an obsolete company, mid-March
in a Midwestern city where parking lots
loom like an apotheosis of boredom.

It's 9:04 and I'm leaning against the faux
wood wall, texting or plucking the sleeve
from my coffee cup, studiously avoiding
eye contact, when someone—it is you,
Reader—trots toward the elevator,
your stylish yet sensible shoes tapping
like a carriage horse across concrete.
Just as the door beeps and begins to shut
I thrust my arm into harm's way, wanting you
to know how chivalrous I can be. Here we are
together in the elevator, almost touching
in the track lighting's cyanotic glare, fondling
the backs of strangers' heads with our eyes,

wondering which bones they've broken,
who among them are gluten intolerant.

I have dreamed us here a long, hard time,
have conjured the vague salt stains on your
pea coat, the cautionary umbrella jutting
from your tote bag. And you trust me
in a trite way, how courteously I remove
my backpack when it bumps your arm.
My appropriately neutral tone when I ask,
Which floor? The elevator delivers you
to Accounts where a meeting's already started.
One client has cold feet, another's a sure thing,
and your boss would like to speak with you later.
Please close the door.

You want a prettier dream. Of course you do.
And it is my nature to please, to entertain you,
to offer up an afternoon glimpse of cleavage
in the cafeteria, or let a black bra strap
stray over one arm. All right then, an elevator
in Rome, where you've never been
in my dreams. It is Piazza Della Radio
in 2004, the fascist block apartment
where I live with Donella and Silvia,
who are smoking and shaving their legs
in the bathtub, when suddenly, a high,
girlish scream from the elevator shaft.
Emily!

Now we are going somewhere, but to which floor?

And how shall I coax you there? An anecdote,
a folded coat, a café conversation with Emily,
miniature spoon nudging the foam on her latte?
Emily; Canadian, Scandinavian beer hall pinup doll,
catch-all vessel for glib, gorgeous things
I want to swallow whole. Emily, tilting
her head to one side: *Have you tried helmet sex?*
I have not. *Late at night,* she whispers,
he calls me Snow White, he calls me Petit Whore,
and it's the way it should be when you just wear words.
Emily says she envies my olive skin,
my pronunciation; *so Mediterranean.*

Here we are again in the lobby of a dream,
which is about guilt or desire—what else
is there?—and I am tired of trying to
convince you to forgive me for a crime
I haven't confessed yet. Why would a girl
listen to her friend scream, *Aiuto, per favore!*—
trapped for two hours in an ancient elevator?
Why put a pillow over one's face and sleep
the sleep of the condemned until a stranger
calls the maintenance man? How can I explain
myself in a manner that will arouse your
sympathies and leave you on narcoleptic knees?

Allow me to take you to the sixth floor
of a fascist block apartment. Let me show you
a book by Quasimodo, one pair of larger
than regulation sunglasses, 54 photos
of No Loitering signs, two ticket stubs

from Villa Adriana, a gelateria named Ping Pong.
Do these details amuse? Do they say no one
suffered? Or, if they suffered, then surely it was
worth two sweaty hours? Shall I be reticent?
Or ribald? Show you a photo of me at 23,
cupping Venus's tit in a sunlit amphitheatre?
Did you know that on their deathbeds,
Romans often freed their slaves? It was called
manumission. Death was thus an attempt
at releasing momentum, which reminds me

of a ghost story I read long ago, about a man
who dreamed of a hearse with doppelganger driver
gleefully shouting, *There's room for one more!*
How the next day, in the lobby of an uptown bank,
the elevator man grinned and said the very same words.
You know how this ends—a refusal, a snapped
cable, the denial of momentum. Should I go back
to that elevator shaft in Rome and try to calm Emily?
Should I tell her I hate her and want to fuck her,
that help is always almost on the way for beautiful girls?

If intimacy is what we require, then why
am I wearing this extravagant pink garter
and menstruating alone in my bedroom?
If intimacy is honesty, then why do I worry
that I've exceeded maximum capacity? Let us
draw up a contract. I provide the confined space
and the conversation. You name the destination.
I have often wondered, if a cable snaps
in an empty building, if a poem plunges

six stories in the dark, does it make a sound?
Reader, I fear your presence is required. Is there
room for one more? I am willing to resort
to drastic measures—you and I together
in any elevator you want, my face on your face,
hands singing up legs, my voice in your ear
like a madwoman imitating a madwoman:
release me release me release me.

HOLDING PATTERN, LIFTED

No language but our own shabby
inventory—your childhood mattress,
2 chipped mugs, 4 predawn sex acts.

No audience but the anorexic air
of Mexico City. Your neighbor
with the incontinent bulldog was there

on the landing. And the other,
the willowy hairdresser you must've
been fucking, was there on the stoop

appraising my bad bottle job.
Imposter queen becalmed in her
rented coronation barge, I flaunted

what we were like a liability.
Those scandalous four-inch sandals
tore a smile of blisters across my ankles

until I wanted to be carried home
past the construction on Condesa, to let
the jackhammer's throes rattle my jaw.

Cones changed the flow of traffic.
Flight attendants took the newspapers
away before the plane landed.

If I'd known then, husband, that you'd fly
due north to find me gloveless in this
ordinary Midwest of hunting rifles and English,

I might've ambled through the loudest plazas
in earthquake weather, or kissed the hairdresser
with a mouthful of wax and sympathy.

I might've climbed to the rim of the black
volcano and offered the fear I nursed
like a chubby baby to the fire

that will swallow us all, eventually.

IV.

ARS AMATORIA: SO YOU WANT TO MARRY
A FOREIGN NATIONAL

I.
On the flight from Mexico City to Chicago,
carry your love's birth certificate and the necessary divorce decree

II.
(he was not always your love).

III.
It will read *diferencias irreconciliables*.

IV.
Stuff your suitcase with standard issue souvenirs—
bottles of mezcal, rebozos, talavera mugs.

V.
In the customs line, flash your American passport
and a partisan smile.

VI.
A certain nervousness is normal. At such time, you may wish
to recall an image from your trip to the capital—

VII.
a red potted flower frowning on his fire escape; *amor de un rato*.

VIII.
Veil yourself in the pleasure of names, the exactness of their camouflage.

IX.
Once, lifting your thighs with a violence that embarrasses you now,
he called you *gringa, güera, blanquita.*

X.
Certain memories are degrading and thrilling.

XI.
When the customs agent inquires about the purpose
of your trip abroad, answer voraciously
a vacation!

XII.
Grin into the facial recognition scanner.

XIII.
It is not a crime to carry a Mexican citizen's documents,
even if he is a Mexican.

XIV.
In the coming months you will feel like a traitor,
a tragic character, and a humanitarian.

XV.
The American sensibility betrays an ignorance of scale.

XVI.
From an airplane landing at dusk, taillights tourniquet
the Angel of Independence monument,

XVII.
like the lit wagons of pilgrims,

XVIII.

or strands of Christmas lights
manufactured by prisoners in a *laogai*.

XIX.

It has been said that suffering makes free.

XX.

Already you are abandoning the idea of audience.

XXI.

Already the gauche gold wreath in the angel's hand
resembles a bribe and the broken chain in the other,
an admission of guilt.

XXII.

You break it, you buy it.

XXIII.

Months later, before he enters the U.S. on a tourist visa,
there will be some talk about *worst-case scenarios*.

XXIV.

He might, for example, be *turned back* at the border,

XXV.

as if your foreign national were the longest chapter
of a difficult novel about love in a time
of revolution or famine, one

XXVI.

you were reading for a graduate seminar,
discussing with an earnestness that embarrasses you now

XXVII.
the problems of poetics and narrative shifts.

XXVIII.
There will be some talk about *the best course of action.*
If you can afford it, hire a lawyer.

XXIX.
Do not trust the lawyer.

XXX.
Learn the lexicon—*B-2, I-130, I-94, adjustment of status.*

XXXI.
The passive voice, as in *the papers have been prepared,*
connotes a deferral of agency.

XXXII.
Fanned across an I.N.S. agent's desk,
photos of you and your foreign national
kissing in pornographically azure water;
or the warped, refracted image of your joined hands
in the Bean Sculpture in Millennium Park
will resemble aerial shots of a famous heist.

XXXIII.
At 10,000 feet, headlights on the ground look like downed stars.

XXXIV.
In the waiting room of the third government office,
you will invent your own religion.

XXXV.

If you were raised Catholic, you will equate faith
with martyrdom. *Our Lady of the Styrofoam Cups.*
Our Father Who Art in the Radiant Air Conditioner.

XXXVI.

Like the wooden coffin of a confessional booth,
government offices embody a necessity for self-censorship.

XXXVII.

The thing about air-conditioning, he'll say, *is it doesn't cool
so much as relocate heat.*

XXXVIII.

And air-conditioning will become a covert metaphor
for American imperialism.

XXXIX

In the third government office, it will be easy
to mistake panic for epiphany.

XL.

What is marriage, but an official translation?

XLI.

Are we really pondering the immortality of Octavio Paz?

XLII.

Excuse me, have we provided adequate documentation?
Is our union bona fide?

XLIII.
At the end of his life, Paz professed a preference
for moral over aesthetic endings.

XLIV.
Please review our application materials.
We trust that your verdict will be favorable.

XLX.
From an airplane window, a procession of cars
on the ground might be a wedding
or a funeral. Once,

XLVI.
you believed in beauty
as mystery. Once,

XLVII.
you believed that mystery made the moral
invisible. In the third government office,
you will realize

XLVIII.
your past self was full of shit.

XLIX.
Why are we here?

L.
(Ah, the first person plural.)

LI.

Before you can answer: *I came here for you,*
not winter, not the twenty-minute car rides
to everywhere; not the garish grocery stores
stuffed with unripe fruit.

LII.

Permission is not in itself a destination—
every flight ends on the ground.

LIII.

By now, you will have begun the final descent. Relinquish
your cup and napkin to the stewardess,
who waves a white garbage bag,
like a matador.

LIV.

Like the last scene of a predictable thriller, when
having narrowly averted biological warfare or a coup d'état,
the two stunning undercover agents
kiss and abandon their aliases.

LV.

On the ground,
the cars will look like cars.

LVI.

Can you live there?

LVII.

Say *yes*: Breakfast followed by

habitual sex, head colds, the scrubbing
of pots, the trimming of shrubs,
wine journals, exposed wooden beams,
and learning the language of attachment parenting.

LVIII.
In the coming months, you will discover
that fear of stasis is the inverse of loneliness.

LIX.
For now, naturalization. For now, ever-after. Let it begin

LX.
on the ground, in the September parking lot
outside the government office; in the naked,
unerotic autumn after audience,

LXI.
a calm like a man and a woman
brushing the first dying leaves from the windshield.

ARS POETICA #40
(THE WORST CASE SCENARIO VERSION)

And then everything pressed the eject button.
I dreamed bookcases collapsing like exhausted
sherpas. I dreamed a hernia, kidney stones
and a weeklong trip with the oven on broil.
I dreamed the terrible weight of suitcases
and airline fees; fire and folk remedies
that led to new afflictions. I dreamed beetles
in surgical masks beating the windowpanes
while we spooned on a bed of concrete
and conspiracy theories. I dreamed
the Portuguese Water Dog that betrayed
the whole academy. I dreamed a media frenzy.
Camera crews arrived. Buses arrived.
I barked and got excited.

I dreamed all the pieces of silverware
I stole from fine restaurants in the 90s
flying back to their 77 rightful drawers
with incriminating stories. I dreamed
the burnished weight of soupspoons
that anchored me to subway poles
and bus seats when you were just a wish
I recited to a floor lamp in the ugliest
borough of a city. I wrote letters
and ate words with my fingers,
as a fugitive should. I believed you'd
listen to me if only the music changed.

When I woke, it was the afternoon
of the eclipse and no one remembered
my name. When I woke, I went to the roof
and banged the pots and pans
to scare myself back into myself.

THERE ARE LOTS OF GUNS HERE—

and we cannot trust the refrigerator.
When I return from the doctor with no
diagnosis you're standing in your underwear
waving a bag of rotting vegetables
like a monstrance. We cannot trust
the radishes in the bag the color
of a sad radish's heart the minute
it's pulled from the ground and the rain
has a voice like a president who cannot
believe something he has just said
about security or debt. We cannot trust
the veteran on the first floor
who stalks the parking lot barefoot
in the rain then backs his truck
into six different spots. We cannot trust
that he hates you for being an immigrant
or that he has a gun but maybe one day
soon we'll dial 911 and I do not think
I could write the transformative elegy
the one that turns from grief
to consolation in memory
to an affirmation of immortality.
Forgive me. There are so many situations
to diffuse that one wonders why
buy fresh produce in the first place.
Let's bury our faces in the parsley.
Let's seal up the day like a body bag.

MONOLOGUE DURING A BLACKOUT

What about a zebra?—suppose
you had to come back as a zebra,
        knowing you'd spend your life
                trampling the savannah with the desperation
        of an Open During Construction sign?

Once, stepping off a plane
onto the blacktop of an ancient city
        where my father was born,
                I smelled burning garbage and understood
        anything can happen. Often,

        it doesn't. The rain stops. We are not
washed away. I do not
        glide down five black flights
                to greet the electric truck. But when
        the air conditioner aches on again, how
blunt, how exquisite. No, I don't
        want to be famous. Yes, the radio—
                a man with the voice of a woman sings
        about a woman. The sky,

        you say, looks darker now. Would you
call white a bright color? Would you
        like Bach better through headphones?—
                I mean the seismic privacy of tiny, angry
        gods beating your middle ear. I mean

to make you dizzy. Here,
run your thumb along my chin
      while two workers shimmy down
                  a high-voltage pole and everything
    that can pass between two people—
pleasure, shock, surveillance—
      the static of it—private or public—draws shut
            like curtains across a first-class cabin.

What I thought in the dark,
forget it. A group of zebras is called
    a harem. We call them black.
            We call them white.

EPITHALAMIUM WITH SWAN SONG

I will not harm our bond of affection by an alien love,
but sometimes I'll wake at 4 a.m.
        to follow the palpitating notes
of a song that makes suffering interesting again
to the edge of the brackish water
        into which I'll wade expecting
to be ravished, except instead the swan
will demand great shredded hunks
        of white bread. And in the world

where you will always be breathing
beside me—a song like honking or hissing,
        a bugling call. And in the world
where blue bathing suit bottoms
will mold on the shower rod,
        remember me

as that skinny girl with Lorcaesque eyes
        who fed you twelve white grapes
one New Year's Eve. Nightly,
        you'll make the international sign
for choking or praying. Nightly,
        I'll feed you my body.
Familiarity will be our first sin.

Notes

"Family Elegy in a Late Style of Fire" is an homage to Larry Levis. Its title and structure are indebted to Levis's "My Story in a Late Style of Fire."

"A Genealogy of the Father" contains passages from Friedrich Nietzsche's *The Gay Science.*

"Ars Poetica #9: (The After-hours Version)" is inspired by Terrance Hayes's "Ars Poetica #789."

In "Lorca Addresses His Sister before Her Wedding," the line "Throw that ring in the water" is from Christopher Maurer's translation of Federico García Lorca's "Marriage Vow" (*Songs,* 1924), as found in *The Collected Poems: A Bilingual Edition* (New York: Farrar, Straus and Giroux, 2002).

"Camino Real" is a response to Joshua Clover's "Radiant City."

The title of *"Ars Amatoria*: So You Want to Marry a Foreign National" is taken from Ovid's *Ars Amatoria,* a book series in three parts, devoted to instructing men in matters of love, courtship, and sex. The poem references Alfred Mac Adam's 1991 interview with Octavio Paz, "The Art of Poetry No. 42," in *The Paris Review,* 119 (Summer 1991).

The title of "Dear Forgiveness," borrows a line from poet Richard Siken's "Litany in which Certain Things Are Crossed Out." It is written in the Golden Shovel form, as it is named after Terrance Hayes' "The Golden Shovel," an homage to the Gwendolyn Brooks poem.

The first line of "Epithalamium with Swan Song" is from Ovid's *Metamorphoses,* Book XIV, "Picus and Canens."

Acknowledgments

Grateful acknowledgment is made to the editors of the following journals in which versions of these poems have been published:

AGNI Online: "Lorca Recalls His First Love"
BETTER: Culture and Lit: "Elevator: A Love Story"
Connotations Press: An Online Archive: "Upon Seeing Simon & Garfunkel Live at the Coliseum"
Contrary Magazine: "Epithalamium Intercepted at the Border"
Diode: "By the Numbers"
Drunken Boat: "*Ars Amatoria*: So You Want to Marry a Foreign National"
A Face to Meet the Faces: An Anthology of Contemporary Persona Poetry: "Lorca's Last Letter to Dalí, August 20, 1936"
Failbetter: "Bestiary," "Dying in an Earthquake in Mexico City"
Indiana Review: "V's Dream on the Plane from Mexico City to Chicago"
jubilat: "Monologue during a Blackout"
The Kenyon Review: "Initiation #5: Lorca"
The Massachusetts Review: "Ten Years Apprenticeship in the Republic of Carnivorous Love"
Memorious: "Camino Real," "There Are Lots of Guns Here—"
The Pedestal: "Deathbed"
The Rumpus: "Family Elegy in a Late Style of Fire"
The Southern Review: "A Short Genealogy of Power Tools"
Spillway: "Lorca Addresses His Sister before Her Wedding"
Sycamore Review: "Creation Myth, 1979 (Reappropriated)"

"Family Elegy in a Late Style of Fire" was reprinted in *The Rumpus Anthology of Original Poetry* (2012) and also featured as part of an interview with poet Brian Brodeur for "How a Poem Happens."

For their patience and editorial genius, I'd like to thank Liz Countryman, Anna Journey, Erin Belieu, Timothy Welch, Tana Welch, Frank Giampietro, and Kyle McCord. Special thanks to Connie Voisine for believing in this book and helping to shape it.

Thank you, Madison, Wisconsin, poets (past and present), for all of the laughter and the zany community: Rebecca Hazelton, Laura Eve Engel, Sean Bishop, Adam Fell, and Matthew Guenette. Thanks also to my students and colleagues at the University of Wisconsin-Platteville. Finally, eternal thanks to my mother, father, and Victor.

The completion of this book was assisted by the generous support of the MacDowell Colony, the Virginia Center for the Creative Arts, the Vermont Studio Center, the Bread Loaf Writers' Conference, the Santa Fe Arts Institute, the University of Wisconsin-Platteville, and the Florida State University.